Why Marry?

D0544551

Text copyright © 1997 Christine and David Winter
This edition copyright © 1999 Lion Publishing

The authors assert the moral right
to be identified as the authors of this work

Published by
Lion Publishing plc
Sandy Lane West, Oxford, England
www.lion-publishing.co.uk
ISBN 0 7459 4126 5

First edition 1997
10 9 8 7 6 5 4 3 2 1 0

A catalogue record for this book is available
from the British Library

Typeset in 12/13 Venetian 301
Printed and bound in Singapore

Why Marry?

Choosing the way you live together

CHRISTINE AND DAVID WINTER

A LION BOOK

Contents

Introduction

'Denis and Sue lived just across the road from us. They'd met at work, fallen in love and decided to live together. Eventually they'd bought their present house, with a joint mortgage.'

In most respects they were exactly like a married couple. But, like many people nowadays, they hadn't bothered about getting married.

But now a baby was on the way, and Sue wanted to have the baby baptized – and also to be (as she put it) 'properly' married. So they asked the vicar to call.

Denis was happy about the baptism, but not very keen about getting married. 'Why bother? Just a lot of fuss and show... and expensive, too. We don't need some fancy ceremony to prove we're together. We're not going to split up – after all, we've got a joint mortgage!'

We then embarked on a fascinating conversation. Denis advanced every possible argument against marriage, while Sue kept saying that all the same, she'd like to be married. Eventually Denis came clean. He wasn't that bothered about being married, it was getting married that choked him. And his real objection to that was that he'd have to wear a suit. Denis played bass in a band, and reckoned he was a smart dresser on stage – but no suits! They were for middle-aged, middle-class business types, not him. Once Denis had been assured that at his own wedding he could wear exactly what he liked, his other arguments simply evaporated. By the time the conversation was over, we'd not only fixed the date for the wedding but agreed that the baby (who would by then be a few months old) could be baptized at the end of the service.

In the event it was a marvellous wedding, very real and moving. Denis wore his stage gear (slightly Country and Western style). They made their vows with tears in their eyes, and then proudly saw their small son welcomed into the fellowship of the Christian Church – a church to which they gave an increasingly real commitment over the following months.

The whole incident made us realize how confused many people are about marriage – about what it is, and what it isn't. And also why they find it difficult to see it as the normal, practical and appropriate way to mark the start of a permanent relationship of love between a man and a woman. So it was Denis and Sue, really, who were the initial causes of this book, because there are a lot of people like them.

Living together

❛I can't see the point in getting married. We're very happy the way we are. What difference can it make? We don't need a piece of paper to prove we love each other, do we?❜

Denis and Sue represent just one situation where people are living together. Of course there are lots of others. Many people live together in relationships that are not permanent, and aren't intended to be, though sometimes one partner hopes they will eventually become so. They don't marry because, quite frankly, that is something which they see as a distant possibility, if at all.

Others see the relationship as permanent, but for a variety of reasons don't regard marriage as a serious option. One couple lived together for many years very contentedly, reluctant (as they put it) to risk marriage, because both of them had had very painful previous marriages.

For many, living together isn't a matter of commitment so much as convenience. After all, if you're sleeping together regularly, why not share a bed every night? And why not share the rent, too? In these situations people aren't looking for permanence. When the relationship ends – when one or the other partner is tired of it, loses interest, or moves away to another place for study or work – they are just as likely to recreate a similar situation with another 'partner'. It's a kind of serial monogamy: one partner at a time, but sometimes quite a few of them!

So the phrase 'living together', or the word 'cohabiting', can mean an enormous variety of things, from something almost identical to marriage to a fairly casual relationship of mutual convenience. In this book we're concerned mostly with people who are living together, or are thinking of living together, in a settled, permanent and committed kind of relationship. They may share a mortgage. They may already have, or are thinking of having, children. But for various reasons they are not married.

We believe that many couples in that situation are put off the whole idea of marriage by a mistaken understanding of what it is and what it involves. They may have taken on board the kind of cynicism about marriage that is common in present-day society, or feel that somehow living together offers a degree of personal freedom which would be denied them in marriage.

In this way, many, many couples are being deprived of the joy, security and commitment that Christian marriage, properly understood, could bring them. If a couple love each other, intend to live together on a permanent basis and would like to have a family, then not only is there nothing 'wrong' with getting married – it might be the most 'right' thing they have ever done!

What marriage is

'We knew we wanted to be together for the rest of our lives. We just felt being married was a way of letting everybody know it, too.'

Marriage began long before there were registrars, churches, bridesmaids, iced cakes – or clergy! In the story in Genesis (the first book of the Bible), Adam and Eve were married without any of those complications. It was simply a matter of their own decision. But some words are used to describe their marriage which were taken by Jesus, thousands of years after they were first written, to explain the central idea of what a marriage is. 'Therefore,' it says, 'a man leaves his father and mother and clings to his wife, and they become one flesh.'

Getting married, in other words, is about moving out of one set of relationships ('father and mother') and moving into a new one. It is simply a decision by a couple that they want to be together in the deepest and most intimate way. And that involves turning away from even their closest existing ties – their parents and home – and 'clinging' to each other. In sexual love they become, in the vivid language of the Bible, 'one flesh' – one person, one entity – a unity of two personalities in one. Jesus added, at this point, 'What God has joined together, let not man divide.' So in marriage a couple create a new relationship, a new family, which is then recognized by other people. And within this union of love and permanence children are born and brought up. That, in a nutshell, is the Bible's picture of marriage.

You will notice that there's no mention of legal requirements, churches, fees or licences. It's not the State or the church or the synagogue that marries a couple. They marry each other. It's their decision, freely made, and doesn't actually require any other participant.

But it isn't a private or secret matter. Marriage is a public and social thing. It isn't enough for the couple simply to regard themselves as married. Society has to recognize it, too. That's why, from the earliest times (well, not quite as early as Adam and Eve!), weddings were always public events. The couple made their commitment, and that created the marriage. But they made it before witnesses – usually before their relatives and friends. In that way, people knew that they were married, and treated them as a married couple.

So if we ask, What is marriage?, we have to begin by saying that it's a personal decision by two people, a man and a woman, to live together permanently in a loving sexual relationship. But then we have to add that it's a public declaration, too. They are saying to their family and friends – and to the wider community – that they are now a married couple, beginning a new family in a new home. In virtually every culture in the world those elements are present in what is recognized as 'marriage'. In Western Christian culture, as in the Jewish culture from which it grew, there is another important element, however. Marriage was the object of prayer – prayer for God's blessing on the bride and groom. We recognize that turning away from one set of relationships and embarking on a new and exclusive one is demanding and difficult. People getting married need God's help! So the blessing of the bride and groom is a lovely and important part of the wedding service. Prayer is not essential to marriage, of course. The essentials are the decision and the declaration, before witnesses – which are the basic elements of a marriage in the Registry office. But it is very much a part of the tradition of marriage which we have inherited.

Marriage as Jesus knew it was essentially a family event. The bride went in a procession from her parents' home to the bridegroom's house. There they exchanged their vows in front of their two families and their neighbours. Then a simple prayer ceremony might follow, either in the home or at the synagogue. What definitely always followed was a party, and it lasted several days. It would have been at just such a wedding party that Jesus turned the water into wine – after all, you can't have much of a party on still water! Some things have never changed, and whatever kind of wedding ceremony people have, anywhere in the world, the event is always marked by eating, drinking and making merry.

And so it should be, because, for all its serious and solemn nature, marriage is something to celebrate. Two people have entered into an agreement – a contract, if you like. But it is a voluntary agreement, a contract of love, not compulsion. They have promised to live together and be faithful to each other for the rest of their lives, totally and without reserve. But that commitment springs from love, not law. Only love can make it work.

Now a commitment of that kind can sound quite frightening. When one couple read the marriage vows for the first time ('For better, for worse, for richer, for poorer, in sickness and in health, to love and to cherish till parted by death') the prospective bridegroom whistled quietly and said, 'Not many get-out clauses, are there?' And of course it is very demanding.

But so is loving someone. You can't really love with limits or escape clauses, can you? Love is a total thing, which asks for a total response. If you love your partner, and want to be with them for the rest of your life, and share with them in the birth and upbringing of your children, then a commitment of this kind is essential.

And so is some outside help! And the best source of that help is the God who invented marriage in the first place. He created us as 'pair-bonders'. He says that it isn't good for people to live alone. He sets the lonely in families. And he wants men and women to enjoy the love and security of being 'one flesh'. The wedding service is intended to put the marriage in the context of that help and support. We'll be looking later on at the whole question of getting married in church.

Why not get married?

'Marriage is an old-fashioned institution for keeping women in their place. Liz and I don't want to buy into all that stuff.'

Talking to people who are living together but have decided not to get married, it's easy to discover the reasons why.

The most common one is that it's simply not necessary. The couple are fully committed to each other and can't see what a ceremony, whether religious or civil, would add to that. Often they have made quite solemn promises to each other to stay together, and even to raise the question of marriage is seen as implying that those promises are somehow not valid. If one partner wants a marriage ceremony, the other often feels that that suggests some doubts or insecurity about the relationship. 'We trust each other,' couples say, almost implying that to go through a wedding ceremony would put that trust in doubt. More practically, they often have a joint mortgage – and you can't be more legally bound together than that!

Another, very different, factor in discouraging marriage is the general insecurity of much modern life. If people don't feel secure in their jobs, or know that they may be sent to work in Dubai or Singapore at a few days' notice, they are understandably reluctant to tie themselves to a relationship which quite possibly wouldn't survive such changes. Surely, they argue, it's better to live with the uncertainty for now, and postpone irreversible decisions until you're in a position to make them.

Very often young people quote the bad experiences of others, especially their own parents. They are aware at first hand of the pain that bad marriages can create. They've seen people trapped in a relationship that had been long dead, hurting each other because they couldn't escape from it. 'We wouldn't want that to happen to us,' they say. 'We wouldn't want to go through what our parents went through.' And with nearly half of all marriages ending in divorce, many people of the younger generation have had first-hand experience as children of the grief it can cause. Why get into something that can cause such pain?

Put off by the fuss?

'My sister's wedding cost an absolute fortune. In fact, dad had to take out a second mortgage on the house to pay for it! It's such a waste for just one day. And at the end of it, she's no more married, really, than Mike and me.'

There's no doubt that the cost of weddings, and all the trappings that go along with them, put many couples off the whole idea. When money is a bit tight, or housing very expensive, it does seem stupid to spend thousands of pounds on a wedding – which is apparently fairly average nowadays. Even if parents are paying, the couple see it as a waste, an extravagant jamboree which is forgotten long before the debts are paid off. They can usually think of about three hundred better things to spend the money on!

And it's not just the money. There's all the fuss: clothes, dresses, invitations, hairdos and so on. There is often hassle over who should be invited, and there's a growing problem over the presence of estranged or divorced parents. Many weddings are very tense affairs, as the couple hope and pray that dad and his ex won't actually come to blows at the reception. Then there's the service, the honeymoon and the speeches... In the face of all this, it's not surprising to see why a couple may be tempted to say, Why bother? Isn't it all a lot of fuss about a simple matter of two people deciding to be together?

Getting married also raises the whole question of the changing role of women. There's no doubt that in most societies until very recently a marriage involved the transfer of the ownership of a woman from her father to her future husband. You can see the relic of this in the strange ritual of the father giving away his daughter, even in a modern wedding service.

Many women, and perhaps an increasing number of men, too, have the feeling that marriage is in some way demeaning to women. It seems to imply that the woman becomes the man's possession; something signified by her wearing his ring. Of course, he often wears her ring nowadays! Nevertheless, far from being a partnership of equals, as they feel their present relationship is, this view of marriage sees it as a form of slavery.

She walks into a trap, even if it is a tender one!

So for these, and probably many other related reasons, marriage has become an increasingly less desirable option for people who are in stable and lasting relationships. To put it crudely, the gains that they can see coming to them from getting married seem to be heavily outweighed by the losses. It would add very little, they feel, and possibly take away a lot.

So they don't bother to get married. Though often one partner, at least, would secretly quite like to be.

What about 'trial marriages'?

'I expect John and I will get married one day. But we want to live together first, to see if it will work.'

Quite a few people live together in order to find out whether or not they could be happily married. Some people like to call these 'trial marriages'. In fact, many, if not most, couples coming to book a church wedding give the same address. Some of them, at least, say that they have been living together to see if they're compatible, or can get on together – which presumably is much the same as a trial marriage.

Of course, there's a great deal of sense in doing your best to make sure you aren't embarking on a marriage for life with someone you would find it difficult to live with. Romantic holidays, candlelit suppers and even long drives in the car don't tell you what his domestic habits are!

Marriages have been wrecked by unsuspected traits in apparently highly suitable partners: insanitary habits, irritating mannerisms, extreme untidiness or lax personal hygiene. It may well be a bit late to find out on your wedding night that your lifetime partner insists on sleeping on the same side of the bed as you have always done! On such apparently trivial matters have relationships been sunk without trace!

In the past, that process of discovering what your potential partner was really like took place during what was rather quaintly called 'courting'. In a close community, where everyone knew everyone and children grew up sharing not only bedrooms but beds, there were few private secrets. Couples did get to know each other very well, while not going as far as living together. And there's not the slightest evidence to suggest that worse marriage choices were made in those days, when living together was usually taboo, than now, when it is more or less the norm.

Still, those were different times, and we must recognize that. And there's no doubt that there were many unhappy marriages that survived simply because of public disapproval of divorce, and also the financial dependence of women on their husbands.

So, do trial marriages – put more simply, does

living together before marriage – help to solve the problem of incompatibility? Would it be a good idea even to encourage couples to live together for a while, to see if there were problems that might damage a possible marriage? One can see the attraction of the idea.

However, and whatever way you look at it, living together without the commitment marriage involves is not a trial marriage, any more than two lengths in the local pool could be called a trial cross-channel swim. In some ways they may look like the same thing, but the distinctive feature – the essential length, as it were – is missing.

Living together may tell you a great deal about a partner; that can't be denied. But it isn't, and by its very nature can't be, a trial marriage. Sadly, many people who have lived together quite happily have found that marriage presents a completely different set of challenges – and have broken up. On the other hand, some couples who have had quite stormy relationships while living together have entered much smoother waters when they have actually taken the step of getting married. For one thing, an element of uncertainty has been removed, and some of us find it very difficult to be at peace with ourselves or with others in an atmosphere of uncertainty.

So a trial marriage isn't necessarily going to ensure you a happy and fulfilled real one... and in any case, as we've argued, to call such a relationship a trial marriage is a bit misleading.

What marriage is not

'Mark and I both had pretty set ideas about what marriage was. It was quite a shock to both of us to find out how wrong we were! It was just different from what we expected: better, but different.'

We've looked at what marriage is, and we've looked at some of the reasons why people decide that it's not for them. Perhaps it would help if we now looked at what marriage is not, because we may then see answers to some of the objections which people raise to the whole idea.

For instance, marriage isn't a religious ceremony, though in many cultures, including our own, it has usually involved one. It's often a surprise to people to be told that the Bible doesn't talk of a wedding as a religious ceremony. In fact, church weddings as we know them today are a relatively modern thing.

In the time of Jesus people got married without involving priests, temple or synagogue. In fact, the whole thing was home-made! As we've seen, the bride went in procession with her bridesmaids from her parents' home to the home of her bridegroom. There they exchanged vows, but the main public feature of the event was the party: that was what you got invited to! Of course, there were prayers as well as the vows, but the heart of Jewish marriage wasn't a religious service but a family and public recognition that the couple were now 'husband and wife'.

It's equally true today. As we'll see later, there are many reasons why a religious service is appropriate, but nobody would suggest that it's essential. People married in a registry office are just as much married as those who have a service in church. It's not the prayers or blessing that make the marriage, but the public vows of the couple. As we correctly put it, they marry each other.

Equally, marriage isn't essentially a legal procedure, though in most countries in the Western world, and most others too, getting married does involve things like registrars, fees, licences and certificates. But they don't actually make the marriage so much as confirm and record that it has taken place.

Again, marriage very emphatically is a public

event, but it's not meant to be a public show. Film stars try to have secret weddings, but you can't have a secret marriage, because then it wouldn't really be a marriage at all. People have to know!

Still, the fact that it's public doesn't mean that it has to be spectacular. You can walk to church, rather than have a limousine or horse-drawn carriage. You can wear what you like. You don't have to have bridesmaids and pages. The bride's mother doesn't have to spend several hundred pounds on a new outfit!

Of course, there's a little streak in all of us that wants to impress our friends and relatives; not just 'keeping up with the Joneses' but going one better. Sadly, that can turn a wedding into an opportunity to flaunt wealth or style. But a couple whose wedding cost £50,000 are no more married than a couple whose wedding cost the bare minimum.

It's very sad that some couples are put off the whole idea of marriage because of a wrong idea about weddings. *Being* married is more important than *getting* married. Of course, it's fun to have a lovely wedding, and no one would begrudge the bride her day in the sunshine. And happy occasions should be marked by all the beauty and generosity of which we are capable. But parents who insist on the works must recognize that sometimes it is that very insistence that deters their children from getting married at all.

So marriage isn't a religious or legal ceremony, and although it must – at some level – be public, it doesn't have to be a show. There are two other misunderstandings of marriage that we ought to think about: that it involves some kind of enslavement of women, and that it's simply a way of making sex respectable.

Is marriage 'slavery' for women?

'I've no intention of getting into an institution that is designed to tie me to the sink, the washing machine and the oven for the rest of my life.'

As we've said, there's no doubt that marriage has been used in the past, including the quite recent past, to make women into possessions of their husbands. But that wasn't in line with the teaching of Jesus, or even of the much-maligned apostle Paul (whose letters to the early church are included in the Bible). They saw marriage as a 'one flesh' relationship, in which there was both freedom and mutual dependence. This is how Paul put it: 'In the Lord, woman is not independent of man, nor is man independent of woman... But everything comes from God.'

The modern marriage service, in all of the churches, recognizes this. It is meticulously equal as between man and woman. Both make exactly the same vows and promises. Both agree to share 'all that they have'. Both offer 'all that they are' to the other. And usually each gives a ring to the other, using identical words. If there is any 'enslavement', it is entirely mutual!

It has to be admitted that the whole idea of the bride's father 'giving her away' is, as we've already mentioned, a relic of the idea that the woman is somehow being transferred from one ownership to another – a bit like a footballer being transferred to another club! In this tradition the father takes his daughter's right hand and gives it to the minister, who then gives it to the bridegroom.

This little ceremony is entirely optional, and if you don't like it, or feel it perpetuates wrong ideas about the role of women, then don't do it! Mind you, it is often the first thing a prospective bride asks about. 'Will dad be able to give me away? He's been looking forward to it ever since I was a little girl!' To be honest, it's unlikely that any modern couple, or even their parents, really think of this part of the traditional wedding service as the enslavement of anybody, but just as a charming way to involve the bride's father in her big day.

Anyway, 'giving away' or not, the modern marriage service reflects the changing understanding of the role of women. There can be no doubt about that. And in the marriage itself, rather than just in the ceremony, it's important that the couple work out this new understanding in practice. Saying words is one thing; actually recognizing equality and freedom is a quite different one, especially when issues of career, money and childcare come into focus.

There's nothing in the marriage service that even hints that the sink, the washing machine and the oven are to be the exclusive concern of the woman. The bringing-up and care of children is seen as the responsibility of both partners. And increasingly couples recognize that a woman as well as a man may have a career which is important to them.

But these problems are probably just as difficult for couples living together as for those who are married. And certainly there is no way in which marriage itself, properly understood, can be blamed when women are not treated fairly. The fault is not in the institution, but in us.

Marriage and sex

'We'd wondered what effect getting married would have on our sex lives. Would it be less exciting – or even become a sort of habit? We needn't have worried. It's even better now!'

Marriage isn't a device for making sex respectable, though again it may have been seen in that way at times in the past. It's true that in the Christian tradition, marriage is seen as the environment created by God for the true enjoyment of sex. As it says in the lovely story of the creation of Adam and Eve, 'The man and woman were naked together, and they felt no shame.' Marriage is also seen as the proper environment for the raising of children. Of course, until recent times a sexual relationship almost inevitably led to the birth of children.

But marriage itself doesn't bestow any right to sex and the Marriage Service offers no hint that it does. The Church of England service talks of the 'joy of their bodily union' as one of the gifts of marriage, to be enjoyed with 'delight and tenderness'. That's a long way from the idea that marriage is some kind of a passport to sexual slavery.

What marriage does offer is a different kind of setting for sex, in which it is much more naturally a part of the relationship rather than the main reason for it. Within the security of home and family, and in the context of a relationship which both parties recognize as permanent, a lot of the tension can be taken out of it.

It can't be denied that marriage is, and always has been, about sex. You could say that the Jewish and Christian view of marriage sees it as a contract between a man and a woman sealed by public recognition and their coming together in physical love. The very phrase 'one flesh', quoted by Jesus from the Old Testament, has strong overtones of sexual unity. So a marriage is not a marriage unless it has been 'consummated'. The dictionary defines that as to 'make perfect or complete' and illustrates its meaning by reference to marriage: 'to complete marriage by sexual intercourse'. So an unconsummated marriage can be annulled, which really means that it is null and void. Just as sex without marriage is an incomplete relationship in the Christian view of things, so is marriage without sex.

Of course, for many couples nowadays it is not so much a question of sex completing the marriage contract as vice versa. All the old jokes about couples on their wedding nights sound rather quaint and innocent to modern ears. Yet more and more couples are coming to believe that there were values in the old approach that have been too lightly abandoned. It may well be that the pendulum will one day start swinging the other way, with a new emphasis on chastity before marriage. But we seem a long way from that at present.

In the present situation it has to be accepted that for many, if not most, couples, the marriage ceremony consummates their sexual relationship, rather than the other way round. While that may not correspond with the traditional view of things, it is certainly better than a total rejection of the whole idea of marriage. Perhaps the order of events is less important than the final result, which is, one must hope, a loving and secure relationship in which sexual love can be enjoyed in the way our Creator intended.

Marriage in church?

'We're not what you might call churchy types, but we just felt that we wanted to make a public statement about our relationship to our relatives and friends. And, I suppose, to God, too, in a way. That's why we chose to be married in church.'

Marriage isn't easy, but neither is growing up, playing the cello, going to work, building friendships or any of a hundred other things that are very well worth doing. Marriage demands a kind of self-denial – a sharing and willingness to compromise – that human beings often find very difficult. So most of us need some outside help.

For some people that comes from parents, though sometimes that is a two-edged sword. Help easily becomes what is seen as interference! Friends can be a help, but they can also be a hindrance. 'Start as you mean to go on,' they'll tell you, implying that you should stake out your rights and requirements from the start. The advice often fails to notice that it takes two people to make a marriage, and one person's 'rights and requirements' might seem like selfish demands to another.

For many couples there is a feeling, however vaguely or incoherently it may be expressed, that God's help might not be a bad idea. Often it lies behind a preference to be married in church. Of course, many people choose a church wedding because the pictures look better, or it's a better setting for the dresses and flowers – or simply because the bride's parents want it that way! But there's no doubt that many couples genuinely and sincerely feel that they need all the help they can get, and the idea of a blessing from God on their wedding day seems very reassuring.

It seems right, too, to make those very solemn vows and promises in the presence of God. Of course, if you don't believe in him, then there's not much point in making promises to him, or seeking his help. But many people who are not religious in a conventional way still feel that at this special moment in life they want to recognize a greater love even than their own, and ask for God's blessing on their own love.

You are not 'more' or 'better' married by having a ceremony in church. Everything necessary to a wedding can happen perfectly well in a registry office. But many couples feel that at the biggest moment of their lives they want something more than a civil ceremony. And if they do, they will find that most Christian ministers will understand their feelings.

The wedding service, in all of the Christian churches, is a very positive and joyful celebration of the creation of a new family. It provides a wonderful setting for the vows, which are made in the name of God. And it surrounds the couple with the love and prayers of their relatives and friends. It is serious, because marriage is a serious step to take, but it's also meant to be enjoyed... and most couples do enjoy it, often more than they expected!

So – why get married?

'Like most couples, we have our ups and downs, but we both feel that the marriage gives us a security we didn't really have when we were just living together.'

There are many reasons why people may choose not to get married, or at any rate not to get married yet. We've considered many of them: money, status, the place of women, personal 'freedom' and so on. But the most frequent reason actually given is that couples can't see any advantage in going to all the trouble and expense of getting married. They can see all the disadvantages, but what are the advantages? What has marriage to offer that is so superior to living together – or simply having a sexual relationship outside marriage?

The most obvious advantage is the security that is meant to be the hallmark of marriage. However much a couple may profess undying love and faithfulness, and the intention of staying together 'till death do us part', all the evidence shows that they are less likely to achieve that outside marriage than within it.

Marriage is a commitment that isn't so vulnerable to swings of moods and feelings. After all, even people who love each other dearly sometimes feel less 'in love', but they're no less married. There's a genuine objectivity about being married: either you are married, or you aren't. And swings of mood and feelings of affection can't alter that. So in one sense, marriage helps to limit the damage caused by our changing moods. They're still there, of course: we feel tired and ratty, or our partner seems insufferably smug about something. But we know, or should do, that underneath all these changing feelings of the moment there is a lifelong commitment. Moods and feelings may be powerful, but they can't erase a solemn promise made for life.

Marriage gives both parties an equal status before the law. However much the media may use the phrase, there is really no such thing in Britain as a 'common law wife', nor has there been for centuries. The law recognizes marriage, and regards those who are not married as single. So outside a legally recognized marriage a wife has no claim on her husband, or vice versa, as of right. It's too late to start regretting that after a relationship has broken up in rancour, recrimination and revenge.

Of course, people try to insure against this by drawing up legal documents about their relationship that will decide who gets what (including the children) should the partnership break up. But that seems a cold way to deal with issues related to respect, consideration and love – and very little different from a pre-planned divorce!

In much the same way, who is your 'next of kin' if you are living together? You might want it to be your partner, but that is not how the law sees it. And you may find that is not how relatives see it, either. Sadly, many people have only discovered this when a partner is seriously ill, or has died.

Of course, when you're in love you think such questions are irrelevant. What has the law got to do with it? And no one is suggesting that people who have come to hate each other should be forced to live together. But when you enter into a serious relationship, probably involving property, and possibly children, too, it's important to know on what basis you stand. If it's 'for ever', then why not seal that promise in a binding and public way? And if it's not, why pretend that it is? That's how people get badly hurt.

We've mentioned children. It's now widely recognized that children are normally best, or most happily raised, within a stable and secure family involving two parents. That's not to say that a single parent can't provide love and security: there are plenty of examples to prove that they can. But by its very nature it is more demanding. Raising children is a responsibility best shared!

But it's too simple to say that ideally a child needs a mother and a father. The child also needs to know that the main people in its life will be there right through childhood. A recent survey by the NSPCC showed that anxiety about this is one of the chief causes of unhappiness among children.

Of course, many cohabiting couples have children and stay together permanently. But many don't – and many more cohabiting couples break up than married couples. Not only that, but children know what marriage is, and the security that it brings to them. How do they feel when they know that their parents, for whatever reason, do not want to make a public and binding commitment to each other?

Marriage has had a bad press over recent years. We have all read about the high divorce rate. We all have friends, neighbours and relatives who have had unhappy, and perhaps even violent, married relationships.

What we are less aware of are all the unhappy consequences of broken relationships outside marriage. There are few articles or television programmes about that. Yet everyday experience offers us the evidence of many lives blighted by living together that went disastrously wrong. Often one partner's expectations turned out to be completely at variance with the other's: 'If I'd known that was what you expected, I'd never have gone into it.'

At least marriage solves that problem! No one, surely, can go into a marriage without realizing that it is on the basis of 'one person, for life'. Each partner is entitled to expect that kind of commitment, and in the wedding service it is put in the clearest and most unambiguous words. If it should go wrong, or break down, it is not the fault of marriage as such, but the failure of one or both parties to it.

The strongest reason of all

'All of those seem to be good, practical reasons why it's a good idea to get married. But the best and most important reason is not just good and practical. It goes to the very heart of who we are and what we are intended to be.'

If human beings are not simply cosmic accidents, but the creation of a loving and good God, then it seems to follow that their lives can only find their complete fulfilment in what he knows is best for them. You could think of it like this. When we buy a product – a washing machine, say, or a video recorder – we get the maker's instructions with it. There is usually no legal or moral compulsion to observe those instructions. After all, it's yours, and you're free to do what you like with it. But we know that the thing only works, or only works properly, when it is run according to the maker's instructions. The person who made it knows how it works!

In the same way, if God is our Maker, then presumably he knows how we work. Of course we are free to ignore his directions and to insist on living our lives exactly as we choose. But if we do, we can't really complain if things don't work out well. Our lives – lives created in the image of God – are only properly run when we follow the Maker's directions. And there is no doubt at all that among them, indeed right at the heart of them, is the principle of lifelong marriage between one man and one woman. The principle was established, Jesus said, 'from the beginning'.

It recognizes our nature as 'pair-bonders'.

It affirms that 'it is not good for us to be alone' and that the deep and loving companionship of marriage is part of the Creator's purpose for us.

It offers a God-given fulfilment to women and to men, not in subordination to each other but as equal partners in a new kind of relationship, which the Bible calls 'one flesh'.

It's not easy, and in some ways it runs counter to some modern ideas about individual freedom. But the one who knows us, knows what is best for us. That is why there is no substitute for marriage, though it has many imitators!

If a man and a woman truly love each other, want to be together and especially if they want to have children, the question is not really 'Why get married?' but 'Why not?'